Guide to a Healthy Dog

T.F.H. Publications
One TFH Plaza
Third and Union Avenues
Neptune City, NJ 07753

This book has been published with the intent to provide accurate and authoritative information in regard to the subject matter within. While every precaution has been taken in preparation of this book, the publisher and author assume no responsibility for errors or omissions. Neither is any liability assumed for damages resulting from the use of the information herein.

ISBN 0-7938-1001-9

Printed and bound in the United States of America

www.tfh.com

Printed and Distributed by T.F.H. Publications, Inc.
Neptune City, NJ

Table of Contents

Profile of the Healthy Dog

Owning the perfect dog rarely happens by accident. It is usually the result of an informed purchase and the owner's attempt to do research on both the breed and the individual dog. There are many steps you can take to ensure that you take home the healthiest dog possible.

Selecting a Healthy Dog

Recently, a survey was conducted to determine whether there were more problems occurring in animals adopted from pet stores, breeders, private owners, or animal shelters. Somewhat surprisingly, there didn't appear to be any major difference in the total number of problems seen from these sources; however, each

Signs of a Healthy Dog

 Eyes—His eyes should be bright, clear, and free of redness, discharge, or inflammation.

Nose—His nose should be moist, not dry or cracked, and free of discharge.

Ears—Both ears should look clean and smell pleasant. There should be no soreness or redness.

Mouth—He should have fresh breath and firm, pink gums with no redness or bleeding. There should be no broken or missing teeth.

Body—When you run your hands over the dog's body, he should show no indication of pain or tenderness. There should be no lumps, bumps, or red spots.

Hind end—This area should be clean and free of any debris. The anal sacs on either side of the opening of the anus should not be swollen.

Coat—His coat should be in good condition and free from mats and any other debris, like flea dirt (little black specs). His skin should not appear dry or flaky.

Legs—When you pick up your puppy's legs gently, there should be no pain or stiffness.

Feet—Check between his toes for lumps, sores, burrs, or any other foreign objects.

source had different kinds of problems. Most veterinarians will recommend that you select a "good breeder," but there is no sure way to identify such an individual. A breeder of champion show dogs may also be a breeder of genetic defects. You must make the determination on a case-by-case basis, using your knowledge to help you identify the reputable places to buy your dog.

In order to get a healthy dog, the best approach is to select a pup from a source that regularly performs genetic screening and has documentation to prove it. Whether you are dealing with a breeder, a breed rescue group, a shelter, or a pet store, your approach should be the same. You want to identify a dog that you can live with and screen it for medical and behavioral problems before you make it a permanent family member. If the source you select has not done the important testing needed, make sure they will offer you a health/temperament guarantee before you remove the dog from the premises

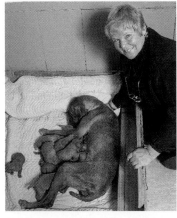

Breeding should be left to people that have experience and knowledge as well as the means to properly care for the mother and the resulting puppies.

BEWARE!

Some breeders will breed puppies purely for profit or out of ignorance. These are often called "backyard" breeders and many of the dogs they breed pass on congenital illnesses or end up in shelters. Watch for these signs of a backyard breeder:

- Breeds many litters a year;
- Has little knowledge about the breed;
- Is not involved in the breed club or in dog sports;
- Claims not to know about or denies genetic problems in the breed or in her line;
- Has no health papers from the veterinarian;
- Will not let you see the whole litter, the place they were raised, or either of the puppy's parents;
- Does not socialize her dogs;
- Asks little or no questions about you or the environment in which the puppy will be raised.

Profile of the Healthy Dog

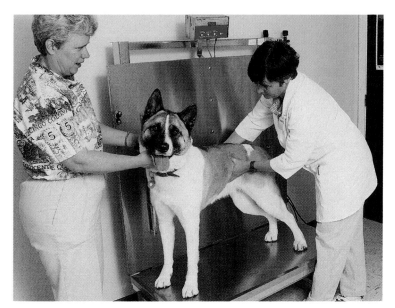

Reputable breeders will screen all their dogs for genetic conditions before breeding them.

to have the work done yourself. If this is not acceptable or if they are offering an exchange-only policy, keep moving; this isn't the right place for you to get a dog. As soon as you purchase a dog, pup or adult, go to your veterinarian for thorough evaluation and testing.

If you are intending to be a pet owner, don't worry about whether your dog is "show quality." A mark here or there that might disqualify the pup as a show winner has absolutely no impact on its ability to be a loving and healthy pet.

Pedigree analysis is best left to true enthusiasts, but there are some things that you can look for, even as a novice. Inbreeding is to be discouraged, so check out your four- or five-generation pedigree and look for names that appear repeatedly. Reputable breeders will usually not allow inbreeding at least three generations back in the puppy's pedigree. Also ask the breeder to provide health certifications for all ancestors in the pedigree. If there are a lot of gaps, the breeder has some explaining to do.

Quick & Easy Guide to a Healthy Dog

What's the OFA?

The Orthopedic Foundation for Animals (OFA) is a non-profit organization established in 1966 to collect and disseminate information concerning orthopedic diseases of animals and establish control programs to lower the incidence of orthopedic diseases in animals. A registry is maintained for both hip dysplasia and elbow dysplasia. The ultimate purpose of OFA certification is to provide information to dog owners to assist in the selection of good breeding animals; therefore, attempts to get a dysplastic dog certified will only hurt the breed by perpetuation of the disease. For more information contact your veterinarian or the Orthopedic Foundation for Animals, 2300 Nifong Blvd., Columbia, MO 65201.

The screening procedure is easier if you select an older dog. Animals can be registered for hip and elbow problems as young as two years of age by the Orthopedic Foundation for Animals (OFA) and by one year of age by Genetic Disease Control

When choosing a puppy, look for one that displays good temperament and a personality that will fit with your family and lifestyle.

(GDC). This is your insurance against hip dysplasia and elbow dysplasia later in your dog's life. If the breeder tells you that they've never heard of these conditions in their lines, it probably means they really don't know if they have a problem and would make them a poor source to find a dog.

Evaluation for genetic or hereditary conditions is somewhat more complicated with puppies. The PennHip™ procedure can determine risk for developing hip dysplasia in pups as young as 16 weeks of age. For pups younger than that, you should request copies of OFA or GDC registration for both parents. If the parents haven't both been registered, their hip and elbow status should be considered unknown and questionable.

For dogs older than one year of age, your veterinarian may also want to take a blood sample to check for thyroid function, heartworm status, and organ function. This will provide a "baseline" for comparison as the dog gets older.

What's the GDC?

The Institute for Genetic Disease Control in Animals (GDC) is a non-profit organization founded in 1990. It maintains an open registry for orthopedic problems but does not compete with OFA. In an open registry like GDC, owners, breeders, veterinarians, and scientists can trace the genetic history of any particular dog once that dog and close relatives have been registered. At the present time, the GDC operates Open Registries for hip dysplasia, elbow dysplasia, and osteochondrosis. The GDC is currently developing guidelines for registries of Legg-Calve-Perthes disease, craniomandibular osteopathy, and medial patellar luxation. For more information, contact the Institute for Genetic Disease Control in Animals, P.O. Box 222, Davis, CA 95617.

Your veterinarian should perform a thorough eye exam on your puppy at his first checkup.

Your veterinarian should also perform a very thorough ophthalmologic (eye) examination. Some common hereditary eye problems in dogs are cataracts, persistent pupillary membranes, glaucoma, and progressive retinal atrophy. It is best to acquire a pup whose parents have both been screened for heritable eye diseases and certified "clear" by organizations such as Canine Eye Registration Foundation (CERF). This is a non-profit organization that screens and certifies purebreds as free of heritable eye diseases. Dogs are evaluated by veterinary eye specialists and their findings are then submitted to CERF for documentation. The goal is to identify purebreds without heritable eye problems so they can be used for breeding. Dogs being considered for breeding programs should be screened and certified by CERF on an annual basis since not all problems are evident in puppies.

Behavioral Screening

Behavioral screening is just as important as medical screening. Gauging your dog's temperament is so important because many

Eyes First

If your pup's parents are certified, an examination by your veterinarian is probably sufficient, and referral to an ophthalmologist is only necessary if recommended by your veterinarian. For more information on CERF, write to CERF, SCC-A, Purdue University, West Lafayette, IN 47907.

dogs are eventually destroyed because they exhibit undesirable behaviors. In fact, more dogs are euthanized each year for behavioral reasons than for all medical problems combined. Temperament testing is a valuable tool in the screening process. Although not all behaviors are evident in young pups (for example, aggression often takes many months to manifest itself), detecting anxiety or fear can be very important in the selection process and will help you avoid choosing a dog that you will not be able to train or live with.

Traits most identifiable in the young pup include: fear; excitability; low pain threshold; extreme submission; and noise sensitivity.

Happy and healthy puppies are a reflection of their breeder's good care. Choose a puppy that is bright-eyed and interested in the world around him.

A puppy's temperament can be evaluated as early as seven to eight weeks of age.

Pups can be evaluated for temperament as early as seven to eight weeks of age. Some behaviorists, breeders, and trainers recommend objective testing where scores are given in several different categories. In general, the evaluation takes place in three stages and is administered by someone the pup has not been exposed to. Also, the testing should not be done within 72 hours of vaccination or surgery.

Temperament Test

In a study conducted in the psychology department of Colorado State University, researchers found that heart rate was a good indicator of puppy temperament. They noted the resting heart rate, stimulated the pups with a loud noise, and measured how long it took the heart rate to recover to resting levels. Most pups recovered within 36 seconds. Dogs that took considerably longer were more likely to be anxious.

A Puppy Aptitude Test (PAT) also can be given to your prospective puppy. In this test, a numerical score is given for responses to 11 different situations, with a "1" representing the most assertive or aggressive expression of a trait and a "6" representing disinterest, independence, or inaction. The traits assessed in the PAT test include social attraction to people, following, restraint, social dominance, elevation (lifting off ground by evaluator), retrieve, touch sensitivity, sound sensitivity, prey/chase drive, stability, and energy level. Although the tests do not absolutely predict behaviors, they do tend to do well at predicting puppies' behavioral extremes.

Feeding and Nutrition

Providing good nutrition is one of the most important aspects of raising a healthy dog, yet it is often the source of much controversy between breeders, veterinarians, pet owners, and dog food manufacturers. First, take a look at the different dog foods available and then determine the needs of your dog.

Commercial Dog Foods

Most dog foods are sold based on marketing, or making a product that appeals to owners while meeting the needs of dogs. Some foods are marketed on the basis of their protein content, some are based on a "special" ingredient, and some are sold because they don't contain certain ingredients (e.g., preservatives, soy). You want a dog food that specifically meets your dog's needs, is economical, and causes few, if any, problems. Most foods come in dry, semi-moist, and canned forms. The dry foods are the most economical, contain the least fat, and the most preservatives. The canned foods are the most expensive (although they're 75 percent water), usually contain the most fat, and have the least preservatives. Semi-moist foods are expensive and are not recommended because they are high in sugar.

Understanding Labels

Although dog food labels tell you a lot about a product, there is a lot they don't tell you. For example, some wording used on labels can be misleading. Foods that use the words "gourmet" or "premium" are not required to contain any higher quality ingredients than any other product. Products that claim to be "all-natural" are not required to be so. Some might think that this means that the food is minimally processed or contains no artificial ingredients, but this is not necessarily true. In fact, all dog foods must contain some chemically-synthesized ingredients in order to be deemed complete and balanced.

When you're selecting a commercial diet, make sure the food has been assessed by using feeding trials for a specific life stage, not just by nutrient analysis. The feeding trial statement is usually located near the ingredient label. In the United States, these trials are performed in accordance with American Association of Feed Control Officials (AAFCO). This certification is important because it has been found that dog foods currently on the market that provide only a chemical analysis and calculated values but no feeding trial may not provide adequate nutrition. The feeding trials show that the diets meet minimal, not optimal, standards; however, they are the best tests currently available.

Your puppy should be fed a good-quality dog food that is nutritious and formulated for his stage of life.

Puppy Requirements

Soon after pups are born and certainly within the first 24 hours of life, they should begin nursing from their mother. This provides them with colostrum, which is an antibody-rich milk that helps protect them from infection for their first few months of life. Pups should be allowed to nurse for at least six weeks before they are completely weaned from their mother. Supplemental feeding may start as early as three weeks of age.

By two months of age, pups should be fed puppy food. They are now in an important growth phase. Nutritional deficiencies and/or imbalances during this time of life are more devastating than at any other time. Also, this is not the time to overfeed pups or provide them with "performance" rations. Overfeeding young dogs can lead to serious skeletal defects such as osteochondrosis and hip dysplasia.

While nursing, your puppy will receive all the nutrients he requires; however, once he is weaned, it is up to you to provide him with the proper nutrition.

Pups should be fed "growth" diets until they are 12 months of age. Pups will initially need to be fed 2 to 3 meals daily until they are 12 months old, then 1 to 2 meals daily (preferably twice) when they convert to adult food. Proper growth diets should be selected based on acceptable feeding trials designed for growing pups. If you can't tell what diet is good for your puppy by reading the label, ask your veterinarian for feeding advice.

Adult Diets

The goal of feeding adult dogs is one of maintenance. They have already done the growing they are going to do and are unlikely to have the digestive problems of elderly dogs. In general, dogs can do well on maintenance rations containing predominantly plant- or animal-based ingredients, as long as that ration has been specifically formulated to meet maintenance level requirements. This contention should be supported by studies performed by the manufacturer in accordance with AAFCO.

There's nothing wrong with feeding a cereal-based diet to dogs on maintenance rations, and they are the most economical diets. Soy is

Supplements

Healthy dogs that are fed a balanced diet will not need supplementation of any kind. In fact, some veterinarians believe that supplementing your puppy's diet with extra vitamins and minerals can aggravate conditions like hip dysplasia and hereditary skin problems. The only time you should ever give your puppy any kind of supplements is under the direction of your veterinarian and then you should never exceed the prescribed amount.

a common ingredient in cereal-based diets but may not be completely digested by all dogs. This causes no medical problems although some dogs may tend to be more flatulent on these diets. When comparing maintenance rations, it must be appreciated that these diets need to meet the minimum requirement levels for confined dogs, not necessarily the optimal levels. Most dogs will benefit when fed diets that contain easily digested ingredients that provide nutrients at least slightly above minimum requirements. Typically, these foods will be intermediate in price, between the most expensive super-premium diets and the cheapest generic diets. Select only those diets that have been substantiated by feeding trials to meet maintenance requirements, those that contain wholesome ingredients, and those recommended by your veterinarian. Don't select a dog food based on price alone, on company advertising, or on total protein content.

Adult dogs should be put on maintenance diets based on their health and levels of activity.

Vegetarian Dogs

Unlike cats, dogs are not true carnivores and can exist on a vegetarian diet. They can convert vegetable fat and protein into the ingredients that they need to perform bodily functions. However, you should consult a veterinarian before switching your dog to a vegetarian diet, because it is a lot of work to maintain balanced nutrition.

Geriatric Diets

Dogs are considered elderly when they are about seven years of age, and their nutritional requirements change as they get older. Your dog's metabolism will slow as he ages and this must be accounted for in his diet. If maintenance rations are fed in the same amounts while his metabolism is slowing, weight gain may result. Obesity is the last thing you want to contend with in an elderly pet, because it increases his risk of developing other health-related problems. As pets age, most of their organs do not function as well as when they were younger.

A dog's needs change drastically between puppyhood and the senior years. Older dogs will need individual attention and special care.

A responsible approach to geriatric nutrition is to realize that degenerative changes are a normal part of aging. Your goal is to minimize the potential damage done by taking this into account while the dog is still healthy. If you wait until your elderly dog is ill before you change his diet, you have a much harder job.

Elderly dogs need to be treated individually. While some benefit from the nutrition found in "senior" diets, others might do better on the highly digestible

Your dog should only be given supplements on the advice of your veterinarian.

puppy and super-premium diets. These latter diets provide an excellent blend of digestibility and amino acid content, but unfortunately, many are higher in salt and phosphorus.

Age and Weight

Older dogs are also more prone to developing arthritis; therefore, it is important not to overfeed them because obesity puts added stress on the joints.

Medical Conditions and Diet

Obesity is the most common nutritional disease afflicting dogs and cats, currently exceeding all deficiency-related diseases combined. Perhaps the pet food companies have done their jobs too well, but the newer foods are probably much tastier to pets than previous ones and encourage overeating. Because many people leave food down all day for free-choice feeding, animals consume more and gain weight. The incidence of obesity increases with age. It is about twice as common in neutered as in nonneutered animals of either sex and, up to 12 years of age, is more common in females than in males. Recent studies indicate that even moderate obesity can significantly reduce both the quality and the length of an animal's life. Fortunately, it is a situation that can be remedied.

It is important to keep in mind that dietary choices can affect the development of orthopedic diseases such as hip dysplasia, osteochondrosis, and intervertebral disc disease. When feeding a dog at risk, avoid high-calorie diets and try to feed several times a day rather than free-feeding. Also avoid supplements of calcium, phosphorus, and Vitamin D, as they can interfere with normal bone and cartilage development. Calcium levels in the body are carefully regulated by hormones (such as calcitonin and parathormone) as well as Vitamin D. Supplementation disturbs this normal regulation and can cause many problems.

Preventive Health Care

Keeping your dog healthy requires preventive health care. This is not only the most effective way to battle illness, but also the least expensive.

Good preventive care starts even before the puppies are born. The mother should be well cared for, vaccinated, and free of infections and parasites. Hopefully, both parents were screened for important genetic diseases, were registered with the appropriate agencies (e.g., OFA, GDC, CERF), showed no evidence of medical or behavioral problems, and were found to be good candidates for breeding. The mother can pass on parasites, infections, genetic diseases, and other health problems if she is not

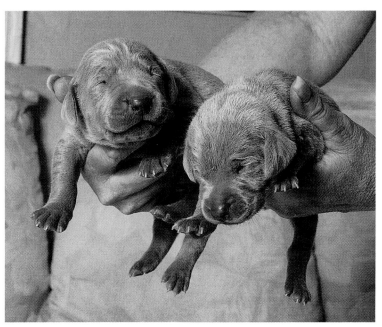

Worms can be passed from mother to puppy; all puppies should be put on a worm control regimen as soon as possible.

healthy. If all has been planned well, the mother will pass on resistance to disease to her pups that will last for the first few months. This gives the pup a good start in life.

Two to Six Weeks of Age

By the second or third week of life, it is usually necessary to start pups on a regimen to control worms. Although dogs benefit from this parasite control, the primary reason for doing this is human health. After whelping, the dam (mother dog) often sheds large numbers of worms, even if she had tested negative previously. This is because many worms lay dormant in tissues, and the stress of delivery causes parasite release and shedding into the environment. You should assume that all puppies have worms, because studies have shown that 75 percent do. Thus, institute worm control early to protect the people in the house and the pups from worms. The deworming is repeated every two to three weeks until your veterinarian feels the condition is under control.

Health Tip

Only use deworming products recommended by your veterinarian. Over-the-counter parasiticides have been responsible for deaths in pups.

Six to Twenty Weeks of Age

Most puppies are weaned from their mother at six to eight weeks of age. Weaning shouldn't be done too early so that the pups have the opportunity to socialize with their littermates and dam. This is important for them to be able to respond to other dogs later in life. There is no reason to rush the weaning process unless the dam can't produce enough milk to feed the pups.

Pups are usually first examined by a veterinarian at six to eight weeks of age, which is when most vaccination schedules commence. If pups are exposed to many other dogs at this young age, veterinarians often opt for vaccinating with inactivated parvovirus at six weeks. When exposure isn't a factor, most veterinarians would

Responsible breeders will start their puppies' vaccination schedules at six to eight weeks of age. You will need to continue this schedule when you take your puppy home.

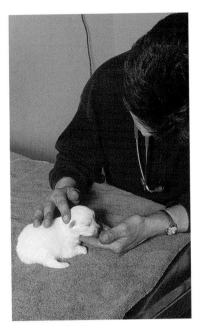

You should take your new puppy to the veterinarian within 48 hours of acquiring him.

rather wait to see the pup at eight weeks. At this point, the veterinarian can also do a preliminary dental evaluation to see that all the puppy teeth are coming in correctly, check to see that the testicles are properly descending in males, and do an examination to determine that there are no health reasons to prohibit vaccination. Heart murmurs, wandering kneecaps (luxating patellae), juvenile cataracts, persistent pupillary membranes (a congenital eye disease), and hernias are usually evident by this time.

Most vaccination schedules consist of injections being given at 6 to 8, 10 to 12, and 14 to 16 weeks of age. Ideally, vaccines should not be given closer than two weeks apart, three to four weeks seems to be optimal. Each vaccine usually consists of several different viruses (e.g., parvovirus, distemper, parainfluenza, hepatitis) combined into

Spaying and Neutering

Some veterinary hospitals recommend neutering pups as early as six to eight weeks of age. A study done at the University of Florida, College of Veterinary Medicine over a span of more than four years concluded there was no increase in complications when animals were neutered when less than six months of age. The evaluators also concluded that the surgery appeared to be less stressful when performed on young pups.

Quick & Easy Guide to a Healthy Dog

Puppy Vaccination Schedule

8 weeks of age—Distemper, hepatitis, leptospirosis, parainfluenza, parvovirus (often given as a combination shot called DHLPP), and Lyme disease.

10 to 11 weeks—Distemper, hepatitis, leptospirosis, parainfluenza, parvovirus, and bordetella

13 to 15 weeks—Distemper, hepatitis, leptospirosis, parainfluenza, parvovirus, and Lyme disease

16 to 18 weeks—Rabies and bordetella

one injection. Coronavirus can be given as a separate vaccination according to this same schedule if pups are at risk. Some veterinarians and breeders advise giving another parvovirus booster at 18 to 20 weeks of age. A booster is given for all vaccines at one year of age and annually thereafter. For animals at increased risk of exposure, parvovirus vaccination may be given as often as four times a year. A vaccine for canine cough (tracheobronchitis), which is squirted into the nostrils, can be given as early as six weeks of age if pups are at risk. A leptospirosis vaccination is given in some geographic areas and likely offers protection for six to eight months. The initial series consists of three to four injections spaced two to three weeks apart, starting as early as ten weeks of age. The rabies vaccine is given as a separate injection at three months of age, repeated when the pup is one year old, then given every one to three years, depending up local risk and government regulation.

Socialization

Between 8 and 14 weeks of age, use every opportunity to expose the pup to as many people and situations as possible. This is part of the critical socialization period that will determine how good a pet your dog will become. This is not the time to abandon a puppy for eight hours while you go to work. This is also not the time to punish your dog in any way, shape, or form.

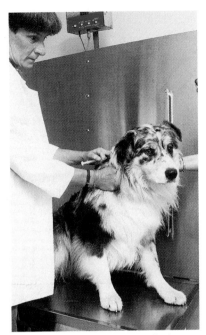

Also, hold off on exposure to other dogs until after the second vaccination in the series. You don't want your new friend to pick up contagious diseases from dogs he meets in his travels before he has adequate protection. By 12 weeks of age, your pup should be ready for social outings with other dogs, and it's a great way for your dog to feel comfortable around members of his own species.

Puppies receive maternal antibodies in the first few weeks of life that protect them from disease; vaccinations are necessary because the antibodies are only temporarily effective.

Identification

Proper identification of your pet is also important, because it minimizes the risk of theft and increases the chances that your pet will be returned to you if he becomes lost. There are several different identification options. Microchip implantation is a relatively painless procedure involving the subcutaneous injection of an implant the size of a grain of rice. This implant does not act as a beacon if your pet goes missing; however, if your pet turns up at a veterinary clinic or shelter and is checked with a scanner, the chip provides information about the owner that can be used to quickly reunite you with your pet. This method of identification is reasonably priced, permanent in nature, and performed at most veterinary clinics.

Another option is tattooing, which can be done on the inner ear or on the skin of the abdomen. Most purebreds are given a number by the associated registry (e.g., American Kennel Club, United Kennel

Club, Canadian Kennel Club, etc.), and this number is used for identification. Alternatively, permanent numbers such as social security numbers (telephone numbers and addresses may change during the life of your pet) can be used in the tattooing process. There are several different tattoo registries maintaining lists of dogs, their tattoo codes, and their owners.

Finally, identifying collars and tags provide quick information but can be separated from your pet if he is lost or stolen. They work best when combined with a permanent identification system such as microchip implantation or tattooing.

Four to Twelve Months of Age

At 16 weeks of age, when your pup gets the last in the series of regular induction vaccinations, ask your veterinarian about evaluating the pup for hip dysplasia with the PennHip™ technique. This helps predict the risk of developing hip dysplasia, as well as degenerative joint disease. Because anesthesia is typically required for the procedure, many veterinarians like to do the evaluation at the same time as neutering.

As a general rule, neuter your animal at about six months of age unless you fully intend to breed the dog. As mentioned earlier, neutering can be safely done at eight weeks of age, but this is still not a common practice. Neutering not only stops the possibility of pregnancy and undesirable

As part of your purchase contract, breeders will usually ask you to spay or neuter your pet-quality puppy.

Preventive Health Care

Heartworm

Incidents of heartworm have been found in all 50 states. According to the American Heartworm Society, the highest infection rate in dogs—up to 45 percent of those not on preventative medication—occurs within 150 miles of the Atlantic and Gulf coasts and along the Mississippi River.

behaviors, but can prevent several health problems as well. It is a well-established fact that pups spayed before their first heat have a dramatically reduced incidence of mammary (breast) cancer. Neutered males significantly decrease their incidence of prostate disorders.

When your pet is six months of age, your veterinarian will want to take a blood sample to perform a heartworm test. If the test is negative and shows no evidence of heartworm infection, the pup will go on heartworm prevention therapy. Some veterinarians recommend preventive therapy in younger pups. This might be a once-a-day regimen, but newer therapies can be given on a once-a-month basis. As a bonus, most of these heartworm preventatives also help prevent internal parasites, such as worms.

Your dog will need regular veterinarian visits to maintain his good health.

Another part of the six-month visit should be a thorough dental evaluation to make sure all the permanent teeth have erupted. If they haven't,

Quick & Easy Guide to a Healthy Dog

this will be the time to correct the problem. Correction should only be performed to make the animal more comfortable and promote normal chewing. The procedures should never be used to cosmetically improve the appearance of a dog used for show purposes or breeding.

One to Seven Years of Age

At one year of age, your dog should be re-examined and receive boosters for all vaccines. Your veterinarian will also want to do a very thorough physical examination to look for early evidence of problems. This might include taking radiographs (x-rays) of the hips and elbows to look for evidence of dysplastic changes. Genetic Disease Control (GDC) will certify hips and elbows at 12 months of age; Orthopedic Foundation for Animals (OFA) won't issue certification until 24 months of age.

Each year, go for another veterinary visit, preferably around the time of your pet's birthday. This visit is a wonderful opportunity for a thorough clinical examination rather than just "shots."

The examination should include visually inspecting the ears, eyes (a great time to start scrutinizing for progressive retinal atrophy, cataracts, etc.), mouth (don't wait for gum disease), and groin; listening (auscultation) to the lungs and heart; feeling (palpating) the lymph nodes and abdomen; and answering all of your questions about optimal health care. In addition, booster vaccinations are given during these times, feces are checked for

Your dog's eyes should always be clear. If they show signs of redness or irritation, visit your veterinarian.

Tooth Care

After the dental evaluation, you should start implementing home dental care. In most cases, this will consist of brushing the teeth one or more times each week and perhaps using dental rinses. It is a sad fact that 85 percent of dogs over four years of age have periodontal disease and doggy breath. In fact, it is so common that most people think it is "normal." Well, it is normal—as normal as bad breath would be in people if they never brushed their teeth. If you brush your dog's teeth regularly with a special toothbrush and toothpaste, you can greatly reduce the incidence of tartar buildup, bad breath, and gum disease. Also, give your dog lots of safe chew toys like Rhinos™ or Dental Chews®.

parasites, urine is analyzed, and blood samples collected for analysis. Other routine blood tests are for blood cells (hematology), organ chemistries, thyroid levels, and electrolytes.

Dental Care

By two years of age, most veterinarians prefer to begin preventive dental cleanings, often referred to as "prophies." Anesthesia is

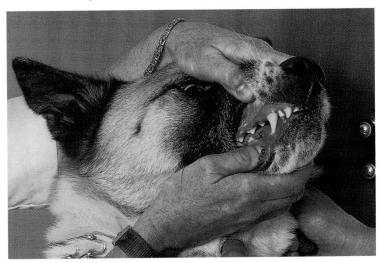

A thorough oral exam should be a part of your dog's annual checkup.

required and the veterinarian or veterinary dentist will use an ultrasonic scaler to remove plaque and tartar from above and below the gum line and polish the teeth so that plaque has a harder time sticking to the teeth. Radiographs (x-rays) and fluoride treatments are other options. It is now known that it is plaque, not tartar, that initiates inflammation in the gums. Because scaling and root planing remove more tartar than plaque, veterinary dentists use a technique called PerioBUD (Periodontal Bactericidal Ultrasonic Debridement). The ultrasonic treatment is quicker, disrupts more bacteria, and is less irritating to the gums. With tooth polishing to finish up the procedure, gum healing is quicker and owners can start home care sooner. Each dog has his own dental needs that must be addressed, but most veterinary dentists recommend prophies annually.

Genetic Problems
Hip Dysplasia
Hip dysplasia is a genetically-transmitted developmental problem of the hip joint that is common in many breeds. Dogs may be born with susceptibility or tendency to develop hip dysplasia, but it is not a foregone conclusion that all susceptible dogs will eventually develop hip dysplasia. All dysplastic

Hereditary problems such as hip dysplasia can be controlled through medical care, diet, and responsible breeding.

dogs are born with normal hips, and the dysplastic changes begin within the first 24 months of life, although they are usually evident long before then.

It is now known that there are several factors that help determine whether a susceptible dog will ever develop hip dysplasia. These include body size, conformation, growth patterns, caloric load, and electrolyte balance in the dog food.

If you start with a pup with less risk of hip dysplasia, you can further reduce your risk by controlling his environ-ment. Select a food with a moderate amount of protein and avoid the super high premium and high-calorie diets. Also, feed your pup several times a day for defined periods rather than leaving the food down all day. Avoid all nutritional supplements, especially those that include calcium, phosphorus, and/or Vitamin D. Use controlled exercise for your pup rather than letting him run loose. Unrestricted exercise in the pup can stress the joints that are still developing.

If you have a dog with hip dysplasia, all is not lost. There is much variability in the clinical presentation. Some dogs with severe dysplasia experience little pain, while others that have minor changes may be extremely sore. The main problem is that dysplastic hips promote degenerative joint disease (osteoarthritis or osteoarthrosis), which can eventually incapacitate the joint. Aspirin and other anti-inflammatory agents are suitable in the early stages; surgery is needed when animals are in great pain, when drug therapy doesn't work adequately, or when movement is severely compromised.

Progressive Retinal Atrophy (PRA)

Progressive retinal atrophy (PRA) refers to several inherited disorders affecting the retina that result in blindness. PRA is thought to be inherited, with each breed demonstrating a specific age of onset and pattern of inheritance.

All of the conditions described as progressive retinal atrophy have one thing in common; there is progressive atrophy or degeneration of the retinal tissue. Night blindness occurs first because the rods, which are responsible for vision in dim light, are affected first. Visual impairment occurs slowly but progressively. Therefore, animals often adapt to their reduced vision until it is compromised to near blindness. Because of this, owners may not notice any visual impairment until the condition has progressed significantly.

Unfortunately, there is no treatment available for PRA, and affected dogs will eventually go blind. Fortunately, PRA is not a painful condition, and dogs do have other keen senses upon which they can depend. Prevention is possible, which is why breeding dogs should be screened annually.

Von Willebrand's Disease

Von Willebrand's disease (vWD) is the most common inherited bleeding disorder of dogs. The abnormal gene can be inherited from

Guide to Life Spans

Your dog will be around for a good number of years, depending on his size and breed. These are average life spans for different types of dogs. Make every year of your dog's life a healthy one!

• Small dogs like Pomeranians, Miniature and Toy Poodles, Shih Tzu, and Yorkshire Terrier—Up to and above 15 years of age

• Medium dogs like Australian Shepherds, Cocker Spaniels, English Springer Spaniels, and Keeshonden—12 to 14 years of age

• Large dogs like German Shepherds, Golden Retrievers Labrador Retrievers, and Rottweilers—10 to 12 years of age

• Giant dogs like Great Danes, Newfoundlands, Great Pyranees, and Saint Bernards—8 to 10 years of age

Guide to a Longer Life

Your job as your dog's caretaker is not over once he receives all his shots. It is very important to take your dog to the vet for an annual checkup, which would include booster vaccinations, a check for intestinal parasites, and a test for heartworm. It is very important for your veterinarian to know your dog in order to give him the best of care, and this is especially true during his middle age on through the geriatric years. The annual physical is good preventive medicine. Through early diagnosis and subsequent treatment of potential problems, your dog can maintain a longer and better quality of life.

one or both parents. If both parents are "clear," none of the pups will be affected. If both parents pass on the gene, most of the resultant pups fail to thrive and die. In most cases, though, the pup inherits a relative

Your dog will rely on you, his owner, to provide him with quality health care.

lack of clotting ability that is quite variable. For instance, one dog may have 15 percent of the clotting factor, while another might have 60 percent. The higher the amount, the less likely it will be that the bleeding will be readily evident, because spontaneous bleeding is usually only seen when dogs have less than 30 percent of the normal level of von Willebrand clotting factor. Thus, some dogs don't get diagnosed until they are neutered or spayed, and

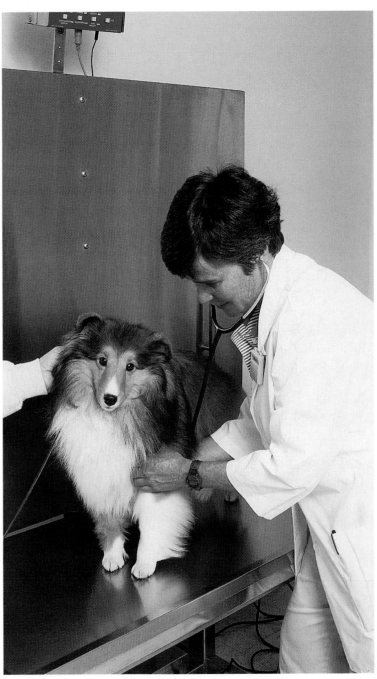

Good health care from the beginning will prevent potential problems and ensure the well-being of your dog.

Preventive Health Care

they end up bleeding uncontrollably or develop pockets of blood (hematomas) at the surgical site.

There are tests available to determine the amount of von Willebrand factor in the blood, and they are accurate and reasonably priced. However, determining carrier status is not straightforward and is very frustrating. Dogs used for breeding should have normal amounts of von Willebrand factor in their blood, and so should all pups that are adopted as household pets. If all breeding animals test "clear," it is not necessary to screen the puppies as well. Carriers should not be used for breeding, even if they appear clinically normal. Since hypothyroidism can be linked with von Willebrand's disease, thyroid profiles can also be a useful part of the screening procedure in the older dog.

Pet Insurance

Statistics show that two out of three pets will experience major medical problems in the course of their lifetime. The high cost of some veterinary procedures, which can run into thousands of dollars, has forced owners that don't have the financial means to make tough decisions. To help defray expenses, more and more owners are turning to insurance for their pets. There are several companies throughout the US that offer this type of insurance. Veterinary Pet Insurance (VPI) is the largest, with more than 850,000 clients. It operates just like a traditional human health care insurance plan. Owners can go to any licensed veterinarian, veterinary specialist, or animal hospital in the world. To find out more about pet insurance, ask your veterinarian, call VPI at (800) 872-7387, or visit the website at: www.veterinarypetinsurance.com.

Preventing Infections and Infestations

An important part of keeping your dog healthy is preventing problems caused by parasites and microbes. Although there are a variety of drugs available that can help limit problems, prevention is always the desired option.

Fleas

Fleas are common parasites but not an inevitable part of every pet owner's reality. If you take the time to understand some of the basics of flea population dynamics, control is both conceivable and practical.

Dogs can pick up parasites like fleas and ticks while playing outdoors. Be sure to check your pup's coat thoroughly when he comes in from the outside.

Fleas have four life stages (egg, larva, pupa, adult), and each stage responds to some therapies while being resistant to others. Effective flea control means interfering with the life cycle of the flea, not just trying to kill adult fleas with potent insecticides. Insecticides kill only adult fleas and larvae and have almost no effect on eggs and pupae. Therefore, insecticide-only flea control is rarely effective unless the environment is perpetually saturated with insecticides to catch the fleas when they are in a susceptible portion of their life cycle.

My Dog Has Fleas?

If you aren't sure if your dog has fleas, have him lie down on a solid, light-colored sheet or blanket. Comb his coat thoroughly, especially around his stomach, in his "armpits," and around his tail (these out-of-the-way places are where fleas like to hide). After you have brushed him, let him up and check out the sheet. If there is any residue on the sheet, the brush, or the comb that looks like salt (which are flea eggs) and pepper (which are flea dirt or fecal matter), your dog has fleas.

Flea Combs

A flea comb is a very handy device for recovering fleas from pets. Fleas collected should be dropped into a container of alcohol, which quickly kills them before they can escape. In addition, all pets should be bathed with a cleansing or flea shampoo to remove fleas and eggs. This has no residual effect, however, and fleas can jump back on immediately after the bath if nothing else is done.

Fleas spend all their time on dogs and only leave if physically removed by brushing, bathing, or scratching. However, the eggs that are laid on the animal are not sticky and fall to the ground to contaminate the environment. Your goal must be to remove fleas from the animals in the house, from the house itself, and from the immediate outdoor environment.

Treating the Dog

A major breakthrough in pet treatment has been the introduction of extremely safe and effective new products to kill adult fleas, such as imidacloprid (Advantage™) and fipronil (Frontline®). A single application will kill adult fleas for over one month. Advantage™ is unaffected by exposure to sunlight and is quickly distributed throughout the body surface without being absorbed into the blood stream. These products are extremely safe, and fipronil is even licensed for use in pregnant and lactating bitches as well as puppies. Pyrethrins and pyrethroids (such as permethrin) are safe products with quick flea "knockdown," but do not give flea control for quite as long a period of time.

Treating the Home

Vacuuming is a good first step when cleaning up the household, because it picks up about 50 percent of the flea eggs and also stimulates flea pupae to emerge as adults, a stage when they are easier to kill with insecticides. The vacuum bag should be removed and discarded with each treatment. Household treatment can then

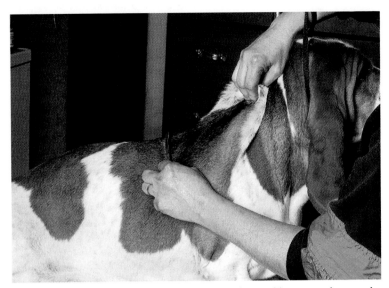

Grooming sessions will help you recognize any skin problems your dog may be experiencing and treat them before they become serious.

be initiated with pyrethrins and a combination of either insect growth regulars or sodium polyborate (a borax derivative). The pyrethrins need to be reapplied every two to three weeks, but the insect growth regulators last about three months to one year, and many companies guarantee sodium polyborate for a full year.

When an insecticide is combined with an insect growth regulator, flea control is most likely to be successful. The insecticide kills the adult fleas, and the insect growth regulator, such as pyriproxyfen, methoprene, and fenoxycarb, affects the eggs and larvae. However, insecticides kill less than 20 percent of flea cocoons (pupae). Because of this, new fleas may hatch in two to three weeks, despite appropriate application of products. This is known as the "pupal window" and is one of the most common causes for ineffective flea control. This is why a safe insecticide should be applied to the home environment two to three weeks after the initial treatment. This catches the newly hatched pupae before they have a chance to lay eggs and continue the flea problem.

Outside Flea Control

Outside flea control is not as difficult as you might think. If you've got a large yard, there's no need to panic. There are some safe and effective things you can do without having to pave your lawn. If you're using a combination of safe adulticide and ovicide/larvicide on all animals in the household, your yard will not be a very fertile ground for new fleas. Routine yard maintenance is one of the most effective ways of managing an outdoor flea problem.

Treat your dog's environment, both inside and outside, to keep him free of parasites.

Insecticide may also be needed in some circumstances; however, it is not necessary to treat the whole yard. Fleas will concentrate in areas that line the patio and garden, shady protected areas, crawl spaces, garages, and around outdoor doghouses. These are the only

Steps to Living Flea-Free

- Vacuum rugs and furniture to get rid of flea eggs. Change the vacuum bag often so fleas are not deposited back into the area later. Treat area with flea killer.

- Wash the dog's bedding and blankets in hot soapy water and wash out all crates, doghouses, toys, etc. with disinfectant.

- Sweep all uncarpeted areas, including porches, sidewalks, and patios.

- Treat yard with flea killer.

- Give your puppy a bath and treat him with topical flea preventative.

- Remember to reapply flea preventative to your dog when needed.

areas that need to be treated. Lawn maintenance will take care of any fleas in the middle of the yard.

> ## Quick and Easy Space Saver
>
> A crate is a very important training tool, and when used properly, can become a second home to your dog. However, that second *home* can take up a lot of space in your *home*, which is why the "Fold-Away Pet Carrier™" is so useful. It's a new kind of crate/carrier combo that's strong enough for airline travel and, when not in use, it easily folds for storage in a closet or under a bed. When you need it, it can be put together in no time.

Ticks

Ticks are found all around the world and can cause a variety of problems including blood loss, tick paralysis, Lyme disease, tick fever, Rocky Mountain Spotted Fever, and babesiosis. All are serious diseases that need to be prevented whenever possible by limiting the exposure of our pets to ticks.

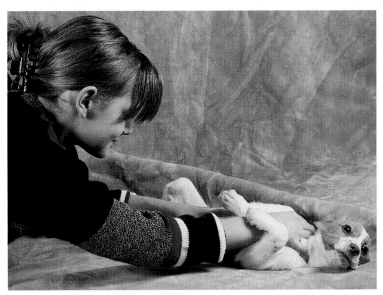

Do a thorough check of your dog's coat on a regular basis.

Lyme Disease

Although it might seem that there should be vaccines for all the diseases carried by ticks, only a Lyme disease *(Borrelia burgdorferi)* formulation is currently available. Ask your veterinarian if it is appropriate to use on your dog.

Ticks feed only on blood, but they don't actually bite. They attach to an animal by sticking their harpoon-shaped mouthparts into the animal's skin, and then they suck blood. Some ticks can increase their size 20 to 50 times as they feed. Favorite places for ticks are between the toes and in the ears, although they can appear anywhere on the skin surface.

A good approach to prevent ticks is to remove underbrush and leaf litter and to thin the trees in areas where dogs are allowed. This removes the cover and food sources for small mammals that serve as hosts for ticks. Ticks must have adequate cover that provides high levels of moisture and, at the same time, provides an opportunity of contact with animals. Keeping the lawn well maintained also makes ticks less likely to drop by and stay.

Because of the potential for ticks to transmit a variety of harmful diseases, dogs should be carefully inspected after walks through wooded areas where ticks may be found, and careful removal of all ticks can be very important in the prevention of disease. Care should be taken not to squeeze, crush, or puncture the body of the tick. Exposure to body fluids of ticks may lead to the spread of any

Ear Cleaning

Never stick anything inside your dog's ear canal. When cleaning, wipe the outside area of the earflap only, or you may damage the dog's eardrum.

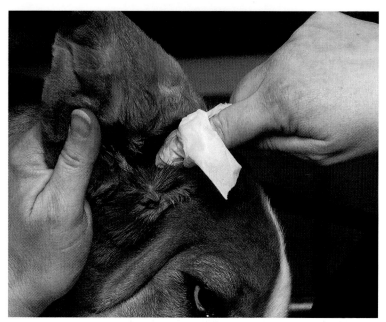

To prevent ear infections and mites, keep your dog's ears clean and free of waxy buildup.

disease carried by that tick to the animal or to the person removing the tick. The tick should be disposed of in a container of alcohol or flushed down the toilet. If the site becomes infected, veterinary attention should be sought immediately.

Mange

Mange refers to any skin condition caused by mites, including include ear mites, scabies mites, Cheyletiella mites, and chiggers, all which are contagious. Demodectic mange is associated with proliferation of Demodex mites, but they are not considered contagious.

The most common causes of mange in dogs are ear mites, which are extremely contagious. The best way to avoid ear mites is to buy pups from sources that don't have a problem with ear mite infestation. Otherwise, pups readily acquire them when kept in crowded environments in which other animals might be carriers. Treatment is effective if whole body (or systemic) therapy is used, but relapses are common when medication in the ear canal is the only approach. This is because the mites tend to crawl out of the ear canal when medications are instilled. They simply feed elsewhere on the body until it is safe for them to return to the ears.

Scabies mites and Cheyletiella mites are contagious, and they can be prevented by keeping your dog away from other dogs that are infested. Scabies (sarcoptic mange) has the dubious honor of being the itchiest disease to which dogs are susceptible. Chigger mites are present in forested areas, and dogs acquire them by roaming in these areas. All can be effectively diagnosed and treated by your veterinarian.

Heartworm

Heartworm disease is caused by the worm *Dirofilaria immitis* and is spread by mosquitoes. The female heartworms produce microfilariae (baby worms) that circulate in the bloodstream, waiting to by picked up by mosquitoes to pass the infection along. Dogs do not get heartworm by socializing with infected dogs; they only get infected by mosquitoes that carry the infective microfilariae. The adult heartworms grow in the heart and major blood vessels and eventually cause heart failure.

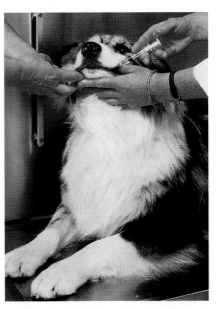

Fortunately, heartworm is easily prevented by safe oral medications that can be administered daily or on a

Your veterinarian will give your dog medication to prevent heartworm and other internal parasites.

Dogs can pick up diseases from other dogs, so be sure that your puppy is fully vaccinated before taking him out to make friends.

once-a-month basis. The once-a-month preparations also help prevent many of the common intestinal parasites, such as hookworms, roundworms, and whipworms.

Intestinal Parasites

The most common internal parasites in dogs are roundworms, hook-worms, tapeworms, and whipworms. Roundworms are the most common. It has been estimated that 13 trillion roundworm eggs are discharged in dog feces every day. Studies have shown that 75 percent of all pups carry roundworms and start shedding them by three weeks of age. People are infected by exposure to dog feces containing infective round-worm eggs, not by handling pups.

Hookworms can cause a disorder known as cutaneous larva migrans in people. They are most dangerous to puppies because they latch onto the intestines and suck blood. They can cause anemia and even death when they are present in large numbers.

The most common tapeworm is *Dipylidium caninum*, which is spread by fleas. However, another tapeworm (*Echinococcus multilocularis*) can cause fatal disease in people and can be spread to people from dogs.

Whipworms live in the lower regions of the intestines. Dogs get whipworms by consuming infective larvae; however, it may be three months before they start shedding them in their stool, greatly complicating diagnosis. In other words, dogs can be infected by whipworms, but fecal evaluations are usually negative until the dog starts passing those eggs three months after being infected.

Other parasites, such as coccidia, cryptosporidium, giardia, and flukes can also cause problems in dogs. The best way to prevent all internal parasite problems is to have pups dewormed according to your veterinarian's recommendations and to have parasite checks done on a regular basis, at least annually.

Viral Infections

Dogs get viral infections such as distemper, hepatitis, parvovirus, and rabies by exposure to infected animals. The key to prevention is controlled exposure to other animals and, of course, vaccination. Today's vaccines are extremely effective, and properly vaccinated

Vaccine Concerns

There are many controversies concerning vaccination, including whether vaccines should be combined in a single injection. Although it's convenient and cheaper to do it this way, might some vaccine ingredients interfere with others? Also, are vaccine schedules designed for convenience or effectiveness? Should the dose of the vaccine vary with weight or should a Chihuahua receive the same dose as a Great Dane? Should some dogs receive higher or lower vaccine dosages than other dogs? Should vets be using modified-live or inactivated vaccine products? For many of these questions, the research is incomplete. There are no short answers for these questions. Ask your veterinarian and do a lot of reading yourself. Ultimately, the choice is yours—you are responsible for the health of your dog.

dogs are at minimal risk for contracting these diseases. However, it is still important to limit exposure to other animals that might be harboring infection. When selecting a facility for boarding or grooming an animal, make sure they limit their clientele to animals that have documented vaccine histories.

Canine Cough

Canine infectious tracheobronchitis, also known as canine cough and kennel cough, is a contagious viral/bacterial disease that results in a hacking cough that may persist for many weeks. It is common wherever dogs are kept in close quarters, such as kennels, pet stores, grooming parlors, dog shows, training classes, and even veterinary clinics. The condition doesn't respond well to most medications, but eventually clears spontaneously over a course of many weeks. Pneumonia is a possible but uncommon complication.

Limiting exposure and utilizing vaccination is the best prevention against this disease. The fewer opportunities you give your dog to come into contact with others, the less the likelihood he will get infected. Vaccination is not foolproof, because many different viruses can be involved.

Parainfluenza virus is included in most vaccines and is one of the more common viruses known to initiate the condition. *Bordetella bronchiseptica* is the bacterium most often associated with tracheobronchitis, and a vaccine is now available that needs to be repeated twice yearly for dogs at risk. This vaccine is squirted into the nostrils to help stop the infection before it gets deeper into the respiratory tract. Make sure the vaccination is given several days (preferably two weeks) before exposure to ensure maximal protection.

First Aid

Every pet owner should be able to help his dog in a medical emergency. This includes being able to take your pet's temperature, monitor pulse and respirations, and to check the capillary refill time (CRT) of the gums. This knowledge can help to save your dog's life.

Temperature

The dog's normal temperature is 100.5 to 102.5 degrees Fahrenheit. Take your dog's temperature rectally for at least one minute. Be sure to shake the thermometer down first, and you may find it helpful to lubricate the end. It is easiest to take the temperature with the dog in a standing position. Be sure to hold

First Aid Kit

Before you bring your puppy home, you should put together a first aid kit, which includes:

• Vital information card with the name, address, and phone number of your vet; name, address, and phone number of the nearest 24-hour emergency veterinary clinic; and the phone number of the National Animal Poison Control Center.

• A muzzle, pantyhose, or stretchable gauze that could be used as a muzzle.

• Scissors

• Tweezers

• Eyewash

• Antibiotic ointment or powder

• Hydrogen peroxide

• Milk of Magnesia

• Thermometer

• Petroleum or other lubricating jelly

• Gauze rolls

• Adhesive bandaging tape

• Cotton balls

• Antibacterial soap

• Blanket or towels

• Rubbing alcohol

on to the thermometer so that it isn't expelled or sucked in. A dog could have an elevated temperature if he is excited or if he is overheated; however, a high temperature could indicate a medical emergency. On the other hand, if the temperature is below 100 degrees, this could also indicate a problem, and your vet should be notified.

Capillary Refill Time and Gum Color

It is important to know how your dog's gums look when he is healthy, so you will be able to recognize a difference if he is not feeling well. There are a few breeds, among them the Chow Chow and its relatives, that have black gums and a black tongue. This is normal. However, in general, a healthy dog will have bright pink gums. Pale gums are an indication of shock or anemia and should be treated as an emergency. Likewise, any yellowish tint to the gums is an indication of a sick dog. To check capillary refill time (CRT), press your thumb against the dog's gum. The gum will blanch out (turn white) but should refill (return to the normal pink color) in one to two seconds. The CRT is very important. If the refill time is slow and your dog is acting sickly, you should call your veterinarian immediately.

Heart Rate, Pulse, and Respirations

Heart rate depends on the breed of the dog and his health. Normal heart rates range from about 50 beats per minute in the larger breeds to 130 beats per minute in the smaller breeds. You can take

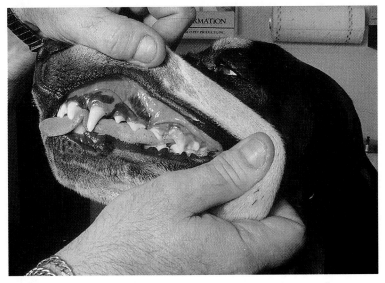

Pale gums can indicate an emergency situation and requires immediate attention.

the heart rate by pressing your fingertips on the dog's chest. Count for either 10 or 15 seconds, and then multiply by either 6 or 4 to obtain the rate per minute. A normal pulse is the same as the heart rate and is taken at the femoral artery located on the insides of both rear legs. Respirations should be observed, and depending on the size

It is important to learn how to take your dog's temperature in case he becomes ill.

and breed of the dog, should be 10 to 30 per minute. Obviously, illness or excitement could account for abnormal rates.

Bleeding

Bleeding can occur in many forms, such as a ripped dewclaw, a toenail cut too short, a puncture wound, a severe laceration, etc. If a pressure bandage is needed, it must be released every 15 to 20 minutes. Be careful when using elastic bandages, because it is easy to apply them too tightly. Any bandage material

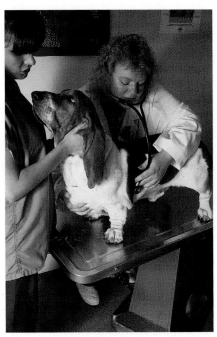

Keep the number of your veterinarian, the emergency clinic, and the poison control center by the phone at all times.

should be clean. If no regular bandage is available, a small towel or washcloth can be used to cover the wound and bind it with a necktie, scarf, or something similar. Styptic powder or even a soft cake of

---

Beware of the Injured Dog

An injured or frightened dog may not even recognize his owner and may be inclined to bite. If your dog is injured, you may need to muzzle him to protect yourself before you try to handle him. It is a good idea to practice muzzling the calm, healthy dog so you understand the technique. Slip a lead over his head for control. You can tie his mouth shut with a two-foot-long bandage or piece of cloth. A necktie, stocking, leash, or even a piece of rope will also work.

First Aid

Keep By The Phone:

It is a good idea to prepare for an emergency by making a list and keeping it by the phone. This list should include:

• Your veterinarian's name, address, phone number, and office hours.

• Your veterinarian's policy for after-hours care. Does she take her own emergencies or does she refer them to an emergency clinic?

• The name, address, phone number, and hours of the emergency clinic your veterinarian uses.

• The number of the National Animal Poison Control Center: 1(800) 548-2423 or 1 (900) 680-0000. It is open 24 hours a day.

soap can be used to stop a bleeding toenail. A ripped dewclaw or toenail may need to be cut back by the veterinarian and possibly treated with antibiotics. Depending on their severity, lacerations and puncture wounds may also need professional treatment. Your first thought should be to clean the wound with peroxide, soap and water, or some other antiseptic cleanser. Don't use alcohol, because it deters the healing of the tissue.

Burns

If your dog gets a chemical burn, call your veterinarian immediately. Rinse any other burns with cold water and if the burn is significant, call your veterinarian. It may be necessary to clip the hair around the burn so it will be easier to keep clean. You can cleanse the wound on a daily basis with saline and apply a topical antimicrobial ointment.

Cardiopulmonary Resuscitation (CPR)

Check to see if your dog has a heartbeat, pulse, and spontaneous respiration. If his pupils are already dilated and fixed, the

If you train your puppy to have good chewing habits and use safe toys such as Nylabones®, he will have healthy teeth throughout his lifetime.

prognosis is less favorable. This is an emergency situation that requires two people to administer lifesaving techniques. One person needs to breathe for the dog while the other person tries to establish heart rhythm. Sometimes, pulling the tongue forward stimulates respiration, but if that does not work, mouth-to-mouth resuscitation starts with two initial breaths, one to one and a half seconds in duration.

Bloat

Although not generally considered a first aid situation, bloat can occur in a dog rather suddenly, and it is an emergency. Gastric dilatation-volvulus or gastric torsion is the twisting of the stomach to cut off both entry and exit, causing the organ to "bloat." It is a disorder primarily found in the larger, more deep-chested breeds. It is life threatening and requires immediate veterinary assistance.

First Aid

After the initial breaths, breathe for the dog once after every five chest compressions (you do not want to expand the dog's lungs while his chest is being compressed). Inhale, cover the dog's nose with your mouth, and exhale gently. You should see the dog's chest expand. You should be ventilating the dog 12 to 20 times per minute. The person managing the chest compressions should have the dog lying on his right side with one hand on either side of the dog's chest, directed over the heart between the fourth and fifth ribs (usually this is the point of the flexed elbow).

Choking

If your dog is choking, first open his mouth to see if any object is visible. If so, remove it. If no object is visible, you can perform the Heimlich maneuver on your dog. Wrap your arms tightly around your dog's belly just under his rib cage. Give one, quick, forceful squeeze, and the object causing the obstruction should be expelled.

Dog Bites

If your dog is bitten by another dog, wash the area and determine the severity of the situation. Some bites may need immediate attention; other bites may be only superficial scrapes. Most dog bite cases need to be evaluated by the veterinarian, and some may require antibiotics. It is important that you learn if the offending dog has had a rabies vaccination. This is important for your dog, but also for you, in case you are the victim. Wash the wound and call your doctor for further instructions. You should check on your tetanus vaccination history, but rarely do dogs get tetanus. If the offending dog is a stray, try to confine him for observation. He will need to be confined for ten days. A dog that has bitten a human and is not current on his rabies vaccination cannot receive a rabies vaccination for ten days.

Eye Care

Red eyes indicate inflammation, and any redness to the upper white part of the eye (sclera) may constitute an emergency. Squinting, cloudiness to the cornea, or loss of vision could indicate severe problems, such as glaucoma, anterior uveitis, and episcleritis. Glaucoma should be considered an emergency if you want to save the dog's sight. A prolapsed third eyelid is abnormal and is a symptom of an underlying problem.

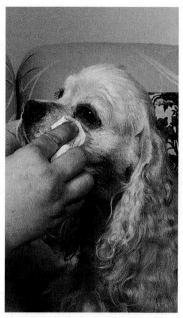

Epiphora and allergic conjunctivitis are annoying and frequently persistent problems. Epiphora (excessive tearing) leaves the area below the eye wet and sometimes stained. The wetness may lead to a bacterial infection. There are numerous causes of this, including

Tearing of the eyes can be caused by many factors, and your veterinarian can determine the best treatment for your dog.

allergies, infections, foreign matter, abnormally located eyelashes and adjacent facial hair that rubs against the eyeball, defects or diseases of the tear drainage system, and birth defects of the eyelids. The treatment is based on the cause.

If something should get in your dog's eye, flush it out with cold water or a saline eye wash. Keeping the hair around the eye cut short and sponging the eye daily will give relief. Many cases are responsive to medical treatment. Allergic conjunctivitis may be a seasonal problem if the dog has inhalant allergies (e.g., ragweed), or it may be a problem year round. The conjunctiva becomes red and swollen and is prone to a bacterial infection associated with mucus accumulation or pus in the eye. Again, keeping the hair around the eyes short will give relief. Mild corticosteroid drops or ointment will also give relief. The underlying problem should be investigated.

No Chocolate!

Dogs like chocolate, but chocolate can kill a dog. Its two basic chemicals, caffeine and theobromine, overstimulate the dog's nervous system. Ten ounces of milk chocolate can kill a 12-pound dog. Symptoms of poisoning include restlessness, vomiting, increased heart rate, seizure, and coma. Death is possible. If your dog has ingested chocolate, you can give syrup of ipecac at a dosage of one-eighth of a teaspoon per pound to induce vomiting and call your veterinarian immediately.

Ingesting Foreign Objects

Most dogs will eat almost anything. All kinds of foreign objects have been removed from a dog's stomach and/or intestinal tract, including socks, pantyhose, stockings, clothing, diapers, sanitary products, plastic, toys, and, last but not least, rawhides. Surgery is costly and not always successful, especially if it is performed too late. If you see or suspect your dog has ingested a foreign object, contact your veterinarian immediately. The vet may tell you to induce vomiting, or she may have you bring your dog to the clinic immediately. Don't induce vomiting without the veterinarian's permission, because the object may cause more damage on the way back up than it would if you allow it to pass through.

Heatstroke

Heatstroke is a serious emergency. The classic signs are rapid, shallow breathing; rapid heartbeat; a temperature above 104 degrees; and subsequent collapse. The dog needs to be cooled as quickly as possible and treated immediately by the veterinarian. If possible, spray him down with cool water and pack ice around his head, neck, and groin. Monitor his temperature and stop the cooling process as soon as his temperature reaches 103 degrees. Keep monitoring his temperature to be sure it doesn't elevate again. If the dog's temperature drops below 100 degrees, it could be life threatening. Get professional help immediately.

Prevention of heatstroke is more successful than treatment. Dogs at the greatest risk are brachycephalic (short-nosed) breeds, obese dogs, and dogs that suffer from cardiovascular disease. Dogs are not able to cool off by sweating as people can. Their only way to cool themselves is through panting and radiation of heat from the skin surface. When stressed and exposed to high environmental temperature, high humidity, and poor ventilation, a dog can suffer heatstroke very quickly. Therefore, you should never leave a dog unattended in a car, even for a few minutes. Also, a brachycephalic, obese, or infirm dog should never be left unattended outside during inclement weather and should have his activities curtailed.

Seizure

Many breeds, including mixed breeds, are predisposed to seizures, although a seizure may be secondary to an underlying medical condition. Usually a seizure is not considered an emergency unless it lasts longer than ten minutes; nevertheless, you should notify your veterinarian. Do not handle the dog's mouth, because your dog probably cannot control his actions and may inadvertently bite you.

Keep your puppy safe and healthy by skipping the table scraps and feeding him only food and treats made for dogs.

Always provide your dog with plenty of cool clean water, especially when outside.

The seizure can be mild; for instance, a dog can have a seizure standing up. More frequently the dog will lose consciousness and may urinate and/or defecate. The best thing you can do for your dog is to put him in a safe place or to block off the stairs or areas where he can fall. Contact your vet to determine the cause of the seizure.

Severe Trauma

If your dog suffers severe trauma, see that his head and neck are extended so if he is unconscious or in shock, he is able to breathe. If there is any vomit, you should try to get the head extended down with the body elevated to prevent the vomit from being aspirated. Alert your veterinarian that you are on your way and get your dog to help immediately.

Shock

Shock is a life-threatening condition and requires immediate veterinary care. It can occur after an injury or even after severe fright. Other causes of shock are hemorrhage, fluid loss, sepsis, toxins, adrenal insufficiency, cardiac failure, and anaphylaxis. The symptoms are a rapid, weak pulse, shallow breathing, dilated pupils, subnormal temperature, and muscle weakness. The capillary refill time (CRT) is slow, taking longer than two seconds for normal gum color to return. Keep the dog warm while transporting him to the veterinary clinic and don't delay—time is critical for survival.

Vaccination Reaction

Once in a while, a dog may suffer an anaphylactic reaction to a vaccine. Symptoms include swelling around the muzzle, extending to the eyes. Your veterinarian may ask you to return to her office to determine the severity of the reaction. It is possible that your dog may need to stay at the hospital for a few hours after future vaccinations.

Poisons

Try to locate the source of the poison (the container that lists the ingredients) and call your veterinarian immediately. Be prepared to give the age and weight of your dog, the quantity of poison consumed, and the probable time of ingestion. Your veterinarian will want you to read off the ingredients. If you can't reach the vet, you can call a local poison center or the National Animal Poison Control Center (NAPCC).

Symptoms of poisoning include muscle trembling and weakness, increased salivation, vomiting, and loss of bowel control. There are numerous household toxins, including pesticides, pain relievers, prescription drugs, plants, chocolate, and cleansers.

Your pet can be poisoned by means other than directly ingesting the toxin. (Ingesting a rodent that has ingested a rodenticide is one example.) It is possible for a dog to have a reaction to the pesticides used by exterminators. If this is suspected, you should contact the exterminator about the potential dangers of the pesticides used and their side effects.

NAPCC

National Animal Poison Control Center is open 24 hours a day. Their phone number is 1(800) 548-2423 or 1 (900) 680-0000. There is a charge for their service, so you may need to have a credit card number available.

Index

Photo Credits

All photographs by Isabelle Francais